PLUTO
AND OTHER DWARF PLANETS

by L. L. Owens

The Child's World

Published by The Child's World®
1980 Lookout Drive • Mankato, MN 56003-1705
800-599-READ • www.childsworld.com

ACKNOWLEDGMENTS
The Child's World®: Mary Berendes, Publishing Director
The Design Lab: Design and production
Red Line Editorial: Editorial direction

PHOTO CREDITS
AP Images, cover, 1, 19, 21, 27, 32; NASA/courtesy of nasaimages.org,
cover, 1, 3, 6, 10, 11, 14, 16, 17, 22, 29, 31; Robert F. Bukaty/AP Images,
5; NASA/courtesy of nasaimages.org/The Design Lab, 6, 7; NASA/JPL/
Univ. of Arizona/courtesy of nasaimages.org, 9; Petr David Josek/AP Images,
13; NASA, ESA, J. Parker (Southwest Research Institute), P. Thomas (Cornell
University), L. McFadden (University of Maryland, College Park), and M.
Mutchler and Z. Levay (STScI)/courtesy of nasaimages.org, 15; Patrick
Reddy/AP Images, 23; Reed Saxon/AP Images, 25

LIBRARY OF CONGRESS CATALOGING-IN-PUBLICATION DATA
Owens, L. L.
 Pluto and other dwarf planets / by L.L. Owens.
   p. cm.
Includes bibliographical references and index.
ISBN 978-1-60954-386-0 (library bound : alk. paper)
1. Pluto (Dwarf planet)—Juvenile literature. 2. Dwarf planets—Juvenile
literature. I. Title.
 QB701.O94 2011
 523.49'22—dc22
                          2010039963

Printed in the United States of America
Mankato, MN
December, 2010
PA02072

ON THE COVER
The Hubble Space Telescope
took this image of icy dwarf
planet Pluto.

Table of Contents

Dwarf Planets and the Solar System

On a clear night, you can see a few planets. Just look up! You might see Mercury or Venus among the stars.

Seeing dwarf planets is not quite so easy. Dwarf planets are smaller planets in the **solar system**. You need a strong **telescope** to see them from Earth.

Jupiter (top), Venus, and the moon are seen from Maine. An airplane streaks across the sky.

SUN

Mercury

Venus

Earth

Mars

Ceres

Jupiter

Fun Facts

OUR SOLAR SYSTEM: Our solar system has eight planets and five dwarf planets. Scientists hope to discover even more dwarf planets in our solar system!

DISCOVERY:
Ceres was discovered on January 1, 1801.
Pluto was discovered in 1930.
Haumea was discovered in 2004.
Makemake was discovered on March 31, 2005.
Eris was discovered in July 2005.

Saturn

Uranus

Neptune

Pluto

Haumea

Makemake

Eris

Planet

Dwarf Planet

What Is a Planet?

Scientists decide what objects in our solar system can be labeled as planets. The number has changed through history as new planets are discovered. To be a planet, the object must be mostly round. It must travel around the sun in a path called an **orbit**. It also must have no similar objects in its orbit.

Jupiter is the largest planet in our solar system.

What Is a Dwarf Planet?

Dwarf planets are round and go around the sun. So why are they called dwarf planets?

Because you will find many objects in a dwarf planet's orbit. For example, many large, icy bodies orbit the sun near Pluto.

Fun Fact

Moons are other round objects in our solar system. But, instead of orbiting the sun, they orbit a planet. This is why they are not dwarf planets. Earth has one moon, but Jupiter has more than 60!

Pluto orbits the sun with other objects in an area named the Kuiper (KY-pur) Belt. An artist created this image of a small Kuiper Belt object.

Scientists formed a **definition** for dwarf planets in 2006. Since then, five dwarf planets have been named. Ceres (SEER-eez) and Pluto have been studied the longest. Haumea (how-MAY-uh), Makemake (MAH-kay-MAH-kay), and Eris (AIR-is) were recent discoveries. But scientists are searching for more dwarf planets.

Scientists voted for the definition of a dwarf planet in Prague, Czech Republic, in 2006.

13

Ceres

Ceres was the first dwarf planet discovered. It orbits between Mars and Jupiter and is the closest dwarf planet to the sun.

In 1801, Italian **astronomer** Giuseppe Piazzi tracked Ceres with his telescope. He thought it was a comet—a smaller, icy object that orbits the sun. Other scientists said it was a planet. Scientists finally labeled Ceres a dwarf planet in 2006.

Fun Fact

Astronomers named Ceres after the Roman goddess of the harvest.

This diagram shows the inner layers of Ceres.

Thin, dusty outer crust

Water-ice layer

Rocky inner core

NASA's Hubble Space Telescope is a giant telescope that was launched into space in 1990. It photographed Ceres. The light gray dwarf planet looks like Earth's moon—but much smaller.

Scientists believe Ceres's center is rocky. The rock may be covered in layers of ice and dust. Scientists also think Ceres has a large ocean. Not many places in our solar system have liquid water.

Fun Fact

NASA stands for the National Aeronautics and Space Administration. It is a US agency that studies space.

The Hubble Space Telescope orbits Earth.

Pluto

In 1930, American astronomer Clyde Tombaugh photographed the sky using a very strong camera. He found Pluto. Pluto was known as the ninth planet, after Neptune, for many years.

But scientists wondered if tiny Pluto should be considered a planet. In 2006, they labeled Pluto a dwarf planet with Ceres. Pluto's switch from planet to dwarf planet was big news. It upset people all over the world!

Clyde Tombaugh sits near the telescope he used to see Pluto.

Scientists say Pluto is cold and very dark. From Pluto, the sun would look about as bright as the moon does from Earth.

Pluto's orbit is more oval than round. Sometimes Pluto travels closer to the sun than Neptune.

The Hubble Space Telescope captured this image of Pluto and one of its moons, Charon.

Haumea

Haumea was discovered in 2004 and was labeled a dwarf planet in 2008. It has an odd shape—more like a football than a baseball. It is made of rock and ice. Haumea has two moons. The moons orbit Haumea as it orbits the sun.

Fun Fact

Haumea was discovered during Christmastime. So until it got its name, scientists called it "Santa."

Large telescopes and **observatories** on Earth allow scientists to study Haumea and other faraway objects without leaving the planet.

Makemake

Makemake was discovered in 2005. It was labeled a dwarf planet in 2008. It is smaller than Pluto. The dwarf planet is very cold—about −400°F (−240°C). That's three times colder than the lowest temperature recorded on Earth!

This special space observatory was placed inside an airplane. It can study the universe in ways telescopes on the ground cannot.

Eris

California astronomers discovered Eris in 2005. It was labeled a dwarf planet in 2006. It is larger than Pluto. Eris is not only the largest dwarf planet. It is also the farthest from the sun.

Eris looks deep gray—the color of the tip of a pencil. Like the other outer dwarf planets, it is cold on Eris. The average temperature is −400°F (−240°C).

An artist created this image of dark-gray Eris, which orbits far from the sun.

Future Exploration

Spacecraft are currently heading toward the outer dwarf planets. In 2015, the *New Horizons* craft will collect details about Pluto's surface and weather.

Scientists hope *Dawn*, another spacecraft, will be able to study any water found on Ceres. All life as we know it needs water. So Ceres may give us important clues about life on Earth and how the solar system formed.

NASA workers prepare the *Dawn* spacecraft for launch.

GLOSSARY

astronomer (uh-STRON-uh-mer): An astronomer is a person who studies planets, stars, or moons. Astronomer Giuseppe Piazzi saw Ceres through his telescope in 1801.

definition (def-uh-NISH-uhn): A definition is a specific explanation or description for something. Scientists formed a definition for dwarf planets in 2006.

observatories (uhb-ZUR-vuh-tor-eez): Observatories are places with telescopes and other tools for studying space. Observatories allow scientists to study faraway objects without leaving Earth.

orbit (OR-bit): To orbit is to travel around another body in space, often in an oval path. Planets and dwarf planets orbit the sun.

solar system (SOH-lur SISS-tum): Our solar system is made up of the sun, eight planets and their moons, and smaller bodies that orbit the sun. Our solar system contains five known dwarf planets.

telescope (TEL-uh-skope): A telescope is a tool that makes faraway objects appear closer. You need a telescope to see the dwarf planets from Earth.

FURTHER INFORMATION

BOOKS

Birch, Robin. *Dwarf Planets*. New York: Chelsea House, 2008.

Landau, Elaine. *Pluto: From Planet to Dwarf*. New York: Children's Press, 2008.

Scott, Elaine. *When Is a Planet Not a Planet?: The Story of Pluto*. New York: Clarion Books, 2007.

Trammel, Howard K. *The Solar System*. New York: Children's Press, 2010.

WEB SITES

Visit our Web site for links about Pluto and other dwarf planets:
childsworld.com/links

Note to Parents, Teachers, and Librarians: We routinely verify our Web links to make sure they are safe and active sites. So encourage your readers to check them out!

INDEX

ABOUT THE AUTHOR

L. L. Owens has been writing books for children since 1998. She writes both fiction and nonfiction and especially loves helping kids explore the world around them.